CW00842320

# Global Leviathan

## BY

## DEREK PHILIP HOUGH

# Global Leviathan

| Chapter | Page |
| --- | --- |
| Hobbes Leviathan. | 1 |
| Current existence of Leviathans and the dream of world peace. | 3 |
| The current level of violence in the world. | 5 |
| The Global Leviathan and democracy. | 9 |
| Democracy vs totalitarianism. | 15 |
| Proposed new world order. | 17 |
| A new definition of democracy. | 20 |
| How a Global Leviathan would view and resolve today's problems. | 23 |

# Hobbes Leviathan

Students of political theory will have already guessed what inspired the choice of the title for this book. Political philosopher Thomas Hobbes published his great work *Leviathan* in 1651. He took the title from the biblical monster mentioned in Isaiah, Job and Psalm 74 of the Old Testament. The political system advocated by Hobbes was based on the idea of a social contract between a strong ruler, the Leviathan, and the people. The people would agree to hand over some of their freedoms (freedom, for example, to take revenge for a perceived wrong) in return for living in a safe and peaceful state. The Leviathan would have a monopoly over law, order and punishments. The people agree in advance to always obey the Leviathan and to accept its decisions. Hobbes' preferred choice of Leviathan was a monarch, but any administrative body could be accommodated into his system. His Leviathan would need to have the best interests of the people at heart otherwise it would risk insurrection and revolt. Hobbes seemed to lean heavily towards a strict Leviathan who we might now view as more of a dictator. His choice of this incredibly powerful monster with its almost obsessive fondness for discipline may have been inspired by a sense of frustration by what he saw around him. Dreadful civil wars had raged in Europe during his lifetime, and he probably concluded that humanity in its natural state could not be trusted to live peacefully. His despair at seeing human behaviour as being 'every man for himself' led him to describe human life as 'solitary, poore, nasty, brutish and short.' Hobbes' political thinking is the most thorough assessment of possible political systems since Aristotle's *Politics*. Strangely enough, after careful consideration, Aristotle also viewed monarchy as the best form of government. Hobbes' view of the natural characteristics of humanity seems to anticipate some interpretations of Darwinism in the nineteenth century. Such expressions as 'nature red in tooth and claw' or 'survival of the fittest' would have been approved of by Hobbes. On the other hand, the eighteenth century left-wing philosopher Jean-Jacques Rousseau, another advocate of the social contract, regarded man in a more natural state as being 'a noble savage.'

When considering the idea of the Leviathan the danger is that a leader who agrees to rule fairly might hijack the machinery of the state and become a brutal dictator. Nietzsche at the end of the nineteenth century viewed the prospect of such a takeover in a favourable light. 'The object is to attain that enormous energy of greatness which can model the man of the future by means of discipline and also by means of the annihilation of millions of the bungled and the botched, and which can avoid going to ruin at the sight of the suffering created thereby, the like of which has never been seen before.'

Hobbes, in his book, gives all manner of advice on how the Leviathan should rule in order to maintain the social contract. There is much to admire in his suggestions. He talks presciently about raising taxes to support the poor and needy. He is an advocate of job creation via expenditure on public works. He argues against any legal system being based on superstition or religious ideas but insists that any legislative body can only be founded on civil law. Similarly, religious revelation experienced by an individual from the past cannot be the basis for law as 'it is manifest that no one can know that they are God's word.' He is not against religion, but he argues against the use of manufactured rituals to support religious obedience. He speaks against the use of saints, demons, relics and images as methods of encouraging religious beliefs. He quite rightly identifies the beneficiaries of superstitious ideas and rituals as being the Church.

## Current existence of Leviathans and the dream of world peace.

The Leviathan concept has proved its worth throughout the world by greatly reducing bloodshed within individual countries. The simple principle is that the Leviathan is authorised to administer the laws of society which have been agreed in advance by the people. The people must agree that the Leviathan will punish them for any transgression even if they themselves fall foul of their own agreed law. Leviathans not only operate in democratic countries, but they maintain peace in totalitarian regimes such as China.

However successful a Leviathan–ruled state seems, there is always the danger of brutal dictatorships or the persecution of minorities within a particular country. We will consider a new definition of democracy to overcome some of the weaknesses of the Leviathan, but the title of this book points to a different type of Leviathan, one that controls the behaviour of different countries in relation to each other. If the Leviathan can work to subdue warlike individuals within each state, then surely, we can be hopeful that a Global Leviathan might subdue warlike states that want to attack other states.

Bertrand Russell in his book *The History of Western Philosophy* explains the English philosopher John Locke's views on the problems of reducing warfare between states.

'If Hobbes' idea for a Leviathan reducing violence within an individual country comes to pass then the problem of man's violence in his *state of nature* is now translated into a violent *state of nature* between individual countries.'

There have been many important historical figures who have championed the idea of some kind of Global Leviathan. Pacifist Albert Einstein was an advocate of a world government. Presumably, he felt that what was needed was an organisation with far more power than the United Nations which has proved ineffective in preventing wars. The United Nations was created in the aftermath of the Second World War. Something had to be tried. Countries in Europe went one step further and commenced the establishment of a Regional Leviathan. For more than sixteen centuries countries in Europe dreamt of a return to Pax Romana but despite the best efforts of Byzantine emperors and charismatic leaders such as Charlemagne and Napoleon, Europe was embroiled in continual slaughter and warfare. Even the psychologically powerful Catholic Church failed to recreate a Roman Empire of the mind. But then in 1957 the European Community became the embryonic precursor of the EU. We should all celebrate the achievement of this Regional Leviathan in keeping the peace.

Again, the pacifist Bertrand Russell explains that another pacifist, the German philosopher Immanuel Kant, in his 1795 treatise on *Perpetual Peace* advocated a federation of free states, bound together by a covenant forbidding war. Reason, Kant says, utterly condemns war, which only an international government can prevent.

Not all philosophers would agree with the need for a war-preventing Global Leviathan. German philosopher Georg Wilhelm Friedrich Hegel for example was against any global authority and thinks that occasional wars are inevitable, necessary, and sometimes morally justifiable. If Fascism ever needed a philosopher, then Hegel is their man. Nietzsche had a similar love of war.

# The current level of violence in the world.

The world is not yet civilised enough to agree to the creation of a war-preventing Global Leviathan and the vision of this new Utopia is a vision of the future. What will be needed to convince humanity to come together is a global catastrophe on a massive scale. Perhaps a nuclear holocaust or an environmental meltdown created by global selfishness. In the future, the population of the world could continue to swell and take humanity right to the brink of such a catastrophe. Just as it took the Second World War to make former enemies think of ways to reduce conflict, a much worse disaster could focus humanity on searching for a better future.

You may be forgiven for thinking that we need the Global Leviathan right now. As I write, wars and major conflicts are raging in the Middle East, The Congo, Myanmar, Sudan and Ukraine but there is statistical evidence that we are now living in the safest and most peaceful period of human history. Steven Pinker in his important book *The Better Angels of Our Nature* uses these statistics to make the point that things were much worse in the past. We might have to gloss over the appalling slaughters of the twentieth century to agree with his assessment, but we would have to agree with him that the vast majority of the human race are not currently living in constant fear of who is coming over the horizon to slaughter them. Autocratic and democratic regimes throughout the world have Leviathans in place to keep the peace within their own states and to encourage good relations between states to reduce the chance of warfare. Not everyone supports Pinker's thesis. One problem which students of the history of violence are faced with is the almost universal propensity of historians, especially ancient historians, to exaggerate the number of deaths in each conflict. According to the Jewish historian Josephus in his history of the Jewish War (66-70 CE) the siege of Jerusalem in 70 CE resulted in 1.1 million deaths. Jerusalem was a city smaller than one kilometre square, and therefore this historically accepted figure is likely to be an exaggeration. It is amazing how these numbers are often nicely rounded up and so, for example, we always read of Genghis Khan slaughtering one million inhabitants of Baghdad. The use of exaggerated numbers of deaths was aimed as a warning to anyone who tried to resist conquest. Killing a million people with swords is hard work, much better that they be terrified into submission instead. Pinker does not help his case by writing 'The worst atrocity of all time was the An Lushan revolt and civil war, an eight-year rebellion during China's Tang Dynasty that, according to censuses, resulted in the loss of two-thirds of the empire's population, a sixth of the world's population at the time.' The number of deaths in this rebellion, according to Pinker was 36 million and pro-rated to the increase in world population is equivalent today of 429 million. In my opinion the true figure for fatalities would have been a small fraction of these numbers.

No-one could argue with the fact that European powers have now stopped killing each other and that the ruthless regimes of Xi Jinping and Putin hardly kill any of their own citizens compared to their monstrous predecessors Mao and Stalin.

The facts bear out that there has been a marked reduction in genocides in recent years, although any genocide makes awful reading. During my own lifetime I have always felt incredibly relieved and lucky that I have never felt the least fear of someone knocking on my door to drag me away for immediate execution or to a period of miserable incarceration before an inevitable death sometime later. My existence has coincided with an age of European peace and prosperity and yet my mental life has been haunted by recurring thoughts relating to The Holocaust and the unresolved mystery, for me anyway, as to how it could have happened. This mystery could easily occupy my thoughts on my deathbed.

Peace reigns in vast areas of the earth's surface but not everywhere, and it is quite common for countries with stable governments to have high levels of criminal murder and there are many non-African countries that suffer ethnic disturbances and bloodshed. However, most continually unstable countries in the world are situated in Africa. It is easier to name the few African countries with histories of long-term stability. Cape Verde, a small country 600 Km from mainland Africa is stable and democratic and the Central African country of Zambia has experienced very little trouble since independence. The most trouble that Zambia has had was a reluctance of its first president, Kenneth Kaunda, to relinquish power but he was soon persuaded to hand over the reins. Another country which is worthy of praise is Botswana. Although there has been some criticism levelled at it for its treatment of the San people, the country is so stable that there is even a TV detective series based there. Other countries are well organised and peaceful despite wars of independence and quasi-democratic administrations. Namibia falls into this category and others such as Kenya and Tanzania have done well despite minor hiccoughs.

As for the other forty-nine countries in Africa here is a list of journalistic expressions or headlines which describe what has gone on there in the past or which goes on there in the present: Military Coup, Tribalism, Ethnic Slaughter, Expulsions, Internally and Externally Displaced People, Preventable Famine, Dictatorships and Family Fiefdoms, Civil Unrest and Mass Demonstrations, Insurrections, Islamist Incursions, Jihadist Inspired Conflict, Mass Executions, Poaching of Rare Animals, Genocides, Ethnic Cleansing, Human Rights Violations, Kidnappings, Independence or Separatist Wars, Violence resulting from Black Magic Beliefs, Violence Against Homosexuals, Female Genital Mutilation, Tourist Murders, Endemic Corruption leading to Failed State Status, Violence resulting from Rigged Elections or Reluctance to Relinquish Power, Environment Destruction leading to Food Shortages etc ,etc. Poor as Africa is, there is always money to buy automatic weapons. Even a casual visitor to somewhere like The Gambia will be struck by the absolute desperation of people to obtain that one or two dollars a day needed to ensure their survival. In some areas of Africa, such as The Democratic Republic of

Congo, Burundi and Rwanda, the death toll can run into millions. Bad as Central Africa is, things are even worse in the Sahel Region. The Economist magazine, in its annual review *The World Ahead - 2024,* writes 'You can walk from the Red Sea to the Atlantic entirely within countries that have had coups in the past three years.' Most of Africa comprises one enormous Basket Case. Enough said!

One of Pinker's explanations for his claimed reduction in warfare and violence is the new thinking engendered by the Enlightenment. A higher moral sense certainly seems to have pervaded human thinking since the days of the burning of witches and the horrors of the Inquisition. It is difficult to say whether evolution has endowed humanity with an in-built moral sense. Our genes are certainly programmed to look after themselves and as copies of our genes are most likely to exist in close relatives then we will almost certainly have an inbuilt instinct to care for our kith and kin. On the other hand, morals are a highly flexible characteristic of humanity. We have seen throughout human history how people are vulnerable to the arguments of the prevailing authorities. Ordinary people can easily be persuaded to commit what would have been previously considered to be acts of evil. A recent example of this manipulation of morals has been observed in Hong Kong. In the former British territory, the police service and the judiciary quickly changed from defending freedoms and democracy to being the main organs of government used to crack down on these freedoms. Whether Steven Pinker's thesis is correct or not we can clearly see that there are not only plenty of slaughters going on around the world but there is also reason to fear the outbreak of a war that could make previous wars look relatively benign.

# The Global Leviathan and democracy.

The principle of the Global Leviathan is the desire to have a world authority that will outlaw war between nations. The Global Leviathan will also demand that each independent country also runs its internal affairs in a fair manner, and we shall consider later what set of rules are needed to eliminate internal warfare. The source of much conflict around the world begins with the internal tyrannies of nation states and these internal problems will have to be addressed by the Global Leviathan with just as much vigour as it applies to conflicts between states.

We will come to the rules demanded by the dreamt-of futuristic Global Leviathan but first let us consider the problems of democracy. In their choice of political systems, democracy has often been the last choice of philosophers down the ages. Winston Churchill also seemed to be sceptical about the efficacy of democracy when he said 'Many forms of government have been tried and will be tried in this world of sin and woe. No one pretends that democracy is perfect or all-wise. Indeed, it has been said that democracy is the worst form of government except for all those other forms that have been tried from time to time.' Needless to say, the insane Friederich Nietzsche was not fond of democracy: 'It is necessary for higher men to make war upon the masses, and resist the democratic tendencies of the age, for in all directions mediocre people are joining hands to make themselves masters.'

According to Aristotle, democracy should never be viewed as acting only in the interests of the needy but must act for all citizens. Aristotle thought that military and economic power often resided in the hands of the self-sufficient citizens and when this group see any possible abuse of democracy by the majority to punish the holders of this military and economic power then this minority will be in a good position, because of its power, to mount a military challenge and this is exactly what happened in Spain in 1936. Aristotle saw limited longevity for any political system and one system would naturally morph into another in a merry-go-round of changing rules. Aristotle feared that within a newly established democracy the more able people will seek enhanced political power and the administration will then become an aristocracy. The privileged aristocrats will then desire to increase their personal wealth and the system will morph into an oligarchy. The oligarchy inevitably descends into a tyranny and then the majority will revolt and fight back to re-create a democracy, and so on.

The twin ideas of the social contract and the Leviathan can be enmeshed into the theoretical ideal of democracy. As has been mentioned previously the citizens get together to make an agreement amongst themselves to obey a set of rules which everyone can admit to being tolerable and then the authority to administer these rules is handed over to a Leviathan. The Leviathan need not be permanent like a hereditary monarch but could be a group of elected officials for the administration of justice. Everyone agrees that the state should be run by a beneficent Leviathan who acts unselfishly for the population.

Despite his misgivings, Aristotle saw the benefits of democracy as creating a system in which various views could be easily absorbed by a large body of people. He thought that a mixture of different desires could result in an overall comprise between different arguments which would then lead to the best outcome. It makes me think of how a work of art, music or literature becomes the most admired. Everyone will see a different element as being appealing and the overall winners in the popularity stakes will emerge as an amalgam of views. Aristotle explains the benefits of democracy by saying that when all the guests contribute to a banquet the outcome will be better than when the food is furnished by a single individual. He then goes on to say that 'a multitude is a better judge of many things than any individual.'

Hobbes concedes that democracy is 'the most natural' form of government and that other advocate of the social contract, Rousseau, seems to concur with this view when he says that a 'mix of opinion' will result in a 'just opinion.' He writes that 'If, when the people, being furnished with adequate information, held its deliberations, the citizens had no communications one with another, the grand total of the small differences would always give the general will, and the decision would always be good.' The key words in the previous quote are 'the citizens had no communications one with another' and for this to be possible, Rousseau sees the need to ban all groups and organisations which could gather for discussions. There can be no societies, religions or political parties. For Rousseau's ideas to work, each individual cannot be influenced by another individual. This sounds very much like the modus operandi of a totalitarian state such as China where groupings of people are very much frowned upon. This isolation is simply not possible in the modern world of social media and people's opinions are at the mercy of anyone who wants to force their ideology onto others.

Full blown democracy is a recent phenomenon and is hardly a hundred years old. How is it faring? For many countries there has only been one free and fair election. After that, the elected leaders have often been reluctant to relinquish power and these leaders have discovered many techniques for holding onto that power. Some regimes merely hold onto power in a despotic way without any thought of fairness and others such as Russia make sure that there is no credible opposition. Another favourite trick is to allow the opposition no publicity at all and to simultaneously flood the public media with stories of how well the government is doing. Populist leaders find out what the major concerns are of most of the population and amend their policies to fit these concerns. The charismatic Boris Johnson persuaded a majority of the British people to vote to be poorer in the Brexit Referendum. There were never going to be any advantages to Brexit. Boris Johnson would have known that there would be no benefits (he is not that

11

unintelligent!) but he didn't care, he just wanted to tell people what they wanted to hear. Sometimes the populist leader can take advantage of a religious majority and demonise any minorities. It is not difficult to reduce or eliminate the chances of an opposition party winning an election.

The greatest threat to democracy in the Western world is the system itself. Populations are fickle, selfish and incredibly vulnerable to fake news. They vote for the party that appears to offer them what they want, and these desires of the population can usually be expressed in monetary terms. People simply want more services and a higher standard of living, and this inevitably puts a strain on public expenditure. Countries throughout the Western world are coming to the limits of what they can afford. The use of a simple spreadsheet model will explain the problem. Sketch out a simple model and let the economy grow at a fixed rate and then allow a government to grow its total expenditure on capital items and on revenue items at the same rate of growth. On the capital side there is a reasonable assumption that we always need to build more and better hospitals, more railways, better roads, new schools, etc, and on the revenue side we always need more doctors and nurses, more teachers, more people to improve the environment and to counter increasing crime. As stated, we can assume that these items of expenditure will increase at the same rate as the economy increases. The spreadsheet will however need an extra column to calculate the extra costs which are then added to future liabilities in the way of the necessary repairs and maintenance to all the capital expenditure that has gone on and also the recent phenomenon of the increasing pension costs of retired public servants who are living longer and are receiving pensions that were never budgeted for. It is quite reasonable to predict that a new school or a new MRI scanner will need continual future expenditure on repairs and maintenance to add to its initial cost. This leads to a gradual exponential, unavoidable increase in necessary public expenditure which is stretching the public finances to the limit. The public debt in the UK is far higher than the published figures.

There is something called 'off-balance sheet financing' and the UK currently has public sector pension liabilities of £2.6 trillion and this enormous liability is not included in the official debt statistics. At election times political parties must promise the electorate more and improved services. No political party could campaign for a curtailing of public services. The UK is a classic case of this problem. Despite increasing wealth, we are now experiencing very high levels of national debt and budget deficits. We can no longer afford to maintain our roads or to run a health service without long waiting times. School buildings are in urgent need of repair. The delays in our legal system are now causing serious concerns, prisons are overflowing, and petty crime has become a major problem due to a lack of policing. Local authorities are desperately short of money. Untreated sewerage is being pumped into our rivers. People are feeling increasingly poor and any enhancement to their wellbeing such as free dental care is now a thing of the past. The average person in the street has no real feeling for the financial problems of the government and all they want is more money to be spent on things which will benefit themselves personally. Populist leaders will take advantage of these problems and tell the electorate what they want to hear, and the danger then is that a leader, who knows full well that they can't deliver on their promises, will hijack the state and refuse to relinquish power. Very few countries around the world have held onto a pure form of democracy and some of them have only survived by increasing their borrowings to keep the electorate happy and even some of these are showing signs of having difficulties with free and fair elections. Even a large portion of the population of that great bastion of democracy the USA is now arguing for an alternative, undemocratic form of government.

It is not only democracies that suffer from a problem with budget deficits. There is no better indicator of a country's political health than the condition of its public services. The world is littered with the ruins of once-amazing cities that are now merely a pile of rubble. Rome would have already been suffering years of neglect by the time it was sacked by the Visigoths in 410 CE and a gradual decline in the condition of the public buildings would have then continued. Even the financial behemoth, China, has dramatically cut back on expenditure on its flagship Belt and Road Initiative. Now that the infrastructure is in place who do the Chinese think is going to maintain it? The Chinese built the TanZam railway across Central Africa to ship copper from Zambia to the port of Dar es Salaam in Tanzania. Its lack of maintenance has made the railway the last choice of the mining companies for the transport of the copper from Zambia's Copperbelt.

# Democracy vs totalitarianism.

Totalitarian states such as Russia, China and Iran do not look admiringly on the Western system. The main difference between the two systems is that open criticism of the government in a totalitarian state is not allowed; you will simply be locked up or worse. In the West, on the other hand, street demonstrations are facilitated by the authorities and national news channels report, on a daily basis, the complaints of the citizens which is a thinly veiled criticism of whichever government is in power. This free speech, which is a cornerstone of democracy, is the main way in which governments are forced to listen to the people. Totalitarian states see democracies as undisciplined and socially disordered. In both systems people can moan about their governments in private around their dinner tables but it is only in democracies that you can moan about your government on the streets. The one thing that both systems have in common however is that discussions about the awfulness of the population and the need to control them take place in private around the dinner tables of the politicians of both democratic and totalitarian regimes. We must never underestimate the level of popular support that Chinese and Russian leaders have amongst their people. Both countries find it very easy to get the population on side when they perceive an actual or an imagined threat from outside. The two prevailing world systems are not as different as we may think. Both democratic and totalitarian states fear popular, uncontrollable uprisings. Mass movements can topple governments in both systems and therefore both are intent on keeping their populations under control by pandering to their demands. Even China had to kowtow to popular anger recently when the government were refusing to lift strict lockdown measures during the coronavirus outbreak. And we all remember Margaret Thatcher backing down from her plans for a Poll Tax at the height of her power. We must never assume that it is only in totalitarian regimes that the people are brainwashed and can be made to do anything. Think back to 1914-18 when young men were easily persuaded to march towards certain death on European battlefields.

# Proposed new world order.

Let us now move onto the proposed rules which all, or at least most, nation states of the world will jointly agree to in order to eliminate global warfare. Both totalitarian and democratic states will have acknowledged the benefits of a Leviathan in maintaining internal order in their own countries and after a massive global catastrophe in which most of the world's population have perished, they might then recognise that what is needed is a Global Leviathan which runs the world with the same authority as they once ran their own countries.

Bertrand Russell acknowledges the need for a Global Leviathan and when discussing the ideas of the social contract as advocated by John Locke in the seventeenth century he writes 'Our age is one of organisation, and its conflicts are between organisations, not between separate individuals. The state of nature, as Locke says, still exists as between states. A new international social contract is necessary before we can enjoy the promised benefits of government. When once an international government has been created, much of Locke's political philosophy will again become applicable.'

Here is an outline of some of the rules of a Global Leviathan.

1. State boundaries will be agreed and fixed in advance and only the Global Leviathan will have the authority to change them.

2. Each individual state will only be allowed weapons such as small arms and light artillery. These weapons can be used as a short term means of defending against a foreign attack before the Global Leviathan can come to the rescue. The Global Leviathan will be absolutely ruthless against an invading army. The armed forces of the transgressor will be entirely eliminated by the highly sophisticated arsenal of weapons held by the Global Leviathan. Hobbes, the originator of the concept of the Leviathan saw the need for this powerful Head of State to brook no disobedience or

argument and whatever the Leviathan does or says is to be taken as Gospel. After all, the rules have been agreed in advance by all participating parties. The Leviathan will run the world with a Machiavellian combination of fairness and an occasional brutal crackdown.

3. The Global Leviathan will have a monopoly over advanced armaments and other technology but the main method of punishing any rogue state who refuses to acknowledge the supremacy of the Global Leviathan will be to totally isolate them from the rest of the world. The rogue state will be hermetically sealed. Technology to prevent any communications between the rogue state and the outside world will be available in the future. There will be only one open, one-way channel of communication and there will be only one acceptable message allowed from inside the sealed state and that message will read 'We surrender.' There will be no trading allowed with the dissenting state, and the rest of the world will not have to suffer the constant stress of hearing upsetting news issuing from the pariah state and the population of the offending state will be left to either starve to death or to kill each other. This harsh treatment is seen as justified by the Utilitarian philosophy of 'the greatest good to the greatest number.'

The idea of isolation is important. In the world in which we currently live, the two opposing types of government, democracy and totalitarianism, still do business together. Neither side is willing to make an economic sacrifice. The West needs cheap manufactured goods from countries such as China. The West is not willing to stop this trade, which would drastically reduce its standard of living, by isolating China as a punishment for its treatment of minorities. In recent years Canada has been one of the few countries in the West to openly criticise both India and China for their behaviour but sadly has received little support from its allies. Nobody wants to upset the economic applecart. The expression *Realpolitik* is often used to justify the 'turning of a blind eye' when observing the human rights violations in totalitarian regimes. Awful countries like North Korea exist simply because other countries such as China and Russia continue to trade with them. Ideally, the world should really split into two halves, each with its own United Nations. The two halves could then be entirely separate, and all countries can choose which self-contained group to belong to. Countries such as Iran, China, Russia, North Korea, Syria and possibly India can form the nucleus of one group and on the other side the United States, the European democracies, Canada, Australia and New Zealand will become founder members of the second group. All other countries of the world can apply to join one side or the other. There need be little or no communication between the groups and the main weapon used by the West against the other group for abuses of human rights will be a total ban on trading links. We are nowhere near ready for such a split, but a future mass catastrophe will convince the world of the sense of using isolation as a means of punishing rogue states.

# A new definition of democracy.

We now come to the desire of the Global Leviathan to prevent or discourage warfare not only between states but also within states. This section is the very *raison d'être* of this small book.

One of the great psychological characteristics of a human being is the desire for control. It is a very important survival mechanism. The young child soon starts testing the boundaries of what is possible when they begin to object to the control which others have over them. In the adult world there are many people who naturally want to be in charge and a few who want to oversee vast numbers of other people and vast areas of territory. In the present day, empires are certainly not a thing of the past. Every capital city in the world with its parliament and administrative district has as its empire all the other areas of the country. Like Rome before them, the client parts of the empire pay a tribute to the centre and the centre can then use these resources as it thinks fit. There are countries today who are still not satisfied with their empires as they currently stand and wish to expand them into other areas outside their current jurisdiction using force if necessary. For the time being, let us remain in the confines of an individual country and consider what really justifies this internal empire. Apart from conquest, what other possible justification is there for the existence of these empires? The one thing that does not justify the ownership of land by these empires is any God-given right to that particular area of land for some historic, geographic or religious reason. Jean-Jacques Rousseau summarises why we finish up where we are by writing 'The first man who, having enclosed a piece of land, bethought himself of saying "this is mine", and found people simple enough to believe him.'

The futuristic Global Leviathan will insist that the borders of countries as they currently exist are frozen and the Global Leviathan will be the only authority able to resolve border disputes. Simultaneously, the place where a particular family or individual currently lives will be then regarded as their

20

legitimate home. The Global Leviathan will take no heed of geographical niceties or historical claims to ownership. The concept of the state fixed onto a certain territory will now be a thing of the past. All the world's land can now be sliced up in a way that suits the people currently calling it their home. It would be totally impractical to make historic claims to any particular territory. People have emigrated and conquered for tens of thousands of years. No group of people could ever have a long-term claim over land otherwise we would all need to leave our homes due to some prior occupation. No. The only fair way to implement the rule of the Global Leviathan is to start with the premise that the current occupier of any particular area of land has a right to live there.

The newly established Global Leviathan will now announce that from now on there will be a new definition of democracy and a new modus operandi which each state is required to adhere to. The great problem with the current definition of democracy rests with the importance of the state as set out in the United Nations Charter. The Charter deals with conflicts between states but does not address the origins of these conflicts which lie within the borders of a state where aggressive policies are hatched. The Charter sees the sovereignty of a state as being sacrosanct and the United Nations washes its hands of any responsibility for the internal affairs of a state. Chapter one, article two, item seven of the Charter clearly establishes this principle: 'Nothing contained in the present Charter shall authorize the United Nations to intervene in matters which are essentially within the domestic jurisdiction of any State or shall require the Members to submit such matters to settlement under the present Charter.' The question therefore is, what set of rules will be needed by the Global Leviathan to do its job? When the Global Leviathan has had time to consolidate its power the world will be given a new definition of democracy which will be not simply *The Rule of the Majority* but will be amended to be defined as *The Rule of the Majority without the Persecution of any Minority*. The state will no longer be sacrosanct, and the area of land occupied by any current state will be entirely divisible when any minority want their own space in which to feel safe. All elections and referendums will be organised by the Global Leviathan who will ensure that all relevant information is presented to the electorate. If any minority can achieve a majority in their chosen area within the boundaries of the present state, then they can choose to be immediately independent. The Global Leviathan will organise the voluntary movement of people between the newly independent state and the old state from which it has broken away. People can choose to live wherever they want, and the Global Leviathan will arrange housing and job swops. There will be no limit to the size of a newly independent state and if any newly independent state then commences to persecute a minority (let's say those that voted against separation) then that minority themselves can carve out a small new state within the borders of the newly independent state. There will be no limit to the number of independent states in the world. There could now be hundreds of thousands of new countries. The military advantage of being part of a large state is now gone. Only the Global Leviathan has any substantial weaponry, and it will always be available to intervene in any small-scale conflict. The ability of any minority to break away from the parent state will encourage the parent state to be ultra-sensitive towards the needs of its minorities as a way of keeping them in the fold. For newly independent states there is no obligation on the part of the parent state to be nice to them and the new state will no doubt be keen to negotiate trade and other agreements with its former parent. At the end of the day the new state might see little difference between independence and their previous status but at least they can now make their own local laws which might better suit their culture.

**How a Global Leviathan would view and resolve today's problems.**

Let us now review the present world and consider how the new definition of democracy would work and how a Global Leviathan could solve some the current world's problems. Remember, this part of the book is a fantasy. There is no chance of any country in the world agreeing to the new definition of democracy but let us pretend that a Global Leviathan is suddenly, magically in place to rule the world. We will start with the United Kingdom and Ireland. The number one rule should be that the people who currently regard the land on which they live as home should have the final say on which country they belong to, or perhaps to choose independence. There is no moral justification for the island of Ireland to be one country. There are plenty of examples around the world of a single island being split between different nations. All the regions of the island of Ireland should be given the chance to be independent states and if such a vote took place today then the outcome would probably be that the six counties of Ulster, voting as one region, would choose to remain within the United Kingdom and all other regions would vote to be part of the Republic of Ireland. However, the Global Leviathan will now apply the new rules of democracy exactly as they were designed to be applied. All the regions of Ulster should now be given another vote, and the Global Leviathan would arrange further referendums within the different regions of Ulster with a view to allowing individual regions to opt to join the Republic. The Global Leviathan would then encourage movements of people so that the two opposing groups could more fairly share Ulster. The logical consequence of the strict adherence to the new rules of democracy would be that the Protestant people of the island of Ireland should finish up with an area of the island in which they have a genuine majority and there is no reason why this arrangement should not last forever. Persecution of any minority would be strictly outlawed under the new definition of democracy and all other regions of the United Kingdom could then also be given the chance for independence. If Yorkshire wanted independence, then it should have it.

The voting patterns of the regions during any referendum on Scottish independence will be scrutinised and no region will be forced to be part of a newly independent Scotland if they don't want to be. The country of Scotland could be broken up with some regions staying within the United Kingdom, some becoming independent and others becoming part of the newly independent country of Scotland. It is quite logical to inform the Scottish National Party that if they think it is moral and reasonable for the people of Scotland to break away from the parent country then it would be equally moral and reasonable for the area around Edinburgh, say, to vote to break away from its newly independent parent at the same time.

All other regions of all other countries around the world can apply to the Global Leviathan to hold an independence referendum. How many of the fifty states of the USA would vote to break away? How many regions of India, each with their own culture and language, would prefer to be independent? The 200 million Muslims who currently feel very insecure and marginalised in Modi's India would be given the chance to carve out numerous independent territories for themselves. Given the choice, Africa would fragment into 1000's of independent kingdoms and the voluntary re-housing of people organised by the Global Leviathan would encourage the creation of new states consisting of single tribes if this is the desired outcome. The Global Leviathan would settle the ethnic wars raging in Myanmar by facilitating the fragmentation of the country into several ethnic states. The Global Leviathan will ensure that empire building comes to an end. Russia would certainly fragment if its people were given a free choice. China would also break up into several regions and the wonderful people of Tibet would then get the chance to reclaim their own culture and language which are currently being systematically erased. It is ludicrous that China is threatening to take by force the island of Taiwan and the reason it can make these threats is because there is currently no Global Leviathan to prevent it. Because we have this obsession, encouraged by the United Nations, of the sanctity of the state then injustices have been allowed to fester for sometimes centuries. It is absurd that the Kurds do not have their own country. The Global Leviathan would act immediately to create a homeland for the Kurds from territory carved out of several countries. There are endless regions of the Middle East and Central Asia which would be best suited to be independent countries. The Global Leviathan would arrange referendums for Catalonia and the Basque Country to determine whether new states should be created. The hundreds of different indigenous peoples of South America and Mexico would welcome the chance to separate from the countries in which they currently find themselves. The Global Leviathan would allocate a small part of South Africa to the European people who consider Africa to be their legitimate home. Currently their culture and way of life are under constant threat, and they could easily suffer the same fate as white Zimbabweans who were ruthlessly chased out of their own country. What would the Global Leviathan do to solve the endlessly intractable problem of Israel and Palestine? The first thing that the Leviathan would do is to ignore the current leaders and influencers on the two opposing sides. The two sides have had a truly hopeless track record of trying to be fair with each other. Injustices from the past will not be taken into account and the Leviathan would start again from scratch and carve up the territory as fairly as it could, taking into account such things as access to fresh water, access to the sea and allocation of good farmland, and would try to link up currently separate areas and build new towns and cities in the two regions. Only a Global Leviathan could solve such a problem.

Emigration, whether forced or natural, has created countries with populations consisting of a mixture of distinct cultures or ethnic groups. People who consider themselves to be a persecuted minority in any country could vote to have a geographic region breakaway to form a new state. The Global Leviathan would also have the power to facilitate the voluntary movement of people into a region where they feel more safe; it is only a matter of housing and jobs. Referendums should be held in the regions illegally seized by Russia in their dispute with Ukraine. If those regions vote to be part of Russia, then that is what should happen and Ukrainians in those regions could be found housing and jobs in the remaining Ukraine. The Global Leviathan would have to be fair and any countries bordering Russia with substantial Russian minorities could also be broken up. One of the consequences of allowing immigrants into your country is that one day their numbers may be sufficient to demand a region of sovereignty for themselves within that country. Indigenous peoples around the world should be given the chance for some element of self-rule, whether it be Native Americans, Māori's or Australia's Aboriginal people. The various peoples of Indonesia and Papua New Guinea would not take too much persuading to go for self-rule. Between these two countries there are thousands of languages and dialects, each reflecting a different culture. Australia would have to listen to demands for independence from groups as diverse as Tasmanians and Torres Strait Islanders.

There still exist throughout the Middle East pockets of religions other than Islam. Most of these minorities have already been eliminated from these regions, but any surviving groups should be given a chance for their own homeland no matter how small. Larger Christian groups in say Lebanon and Egypt will also be given the chance to have their own countries. Central Asian countries also have numerous badly treated minorities, and all these cultural groups will be given a chance to breakaway. An alternative to the creation of a new breakaway state would be for the Global Leviathan to facilitate and finance the voluntary emigration of people from a country where they feel persecuted to a country where they are welcomed. This policy might be usefully applied to the substantial minorities of Russian speaking people of the Baltic States.

The Global Leviathan, armed with the new definition of democracy, will insist that no country has a right to retain within its jurisdiction any minority who want to breakaway. Similarly, no country will have any legitimate claim over a geographic area containing people who want to remain separate. Remember, the key rule is that the people who currently occupy the land have the sole right to determine which country they belong to or to declare themselves independent.

Under the new rules there will be no moral or logical reason why the people of The Falkland Islands or Gibraltar should be forced to change their nationality. As far as the Global Leviathan is concerned history counts for nothing and it is only the current occupiers of these areas who can decide their own future.

There is one situation, long since forgotten by the world, which exemplifies the pathetic weakness of global authorities such the UN to act. It is the former British Protectorate of Somaliland in East Africa. Almost all the people of Somaliland want to be independent of Somalia and various votes have confirmed this and yet the world is just too wedded to the UN obsession with the sanctity of the state to recognise Somaliland as an independent country. Somaliland is therefore left to stagnate as an unrecognised country and is presumably awaiting the arrival of the Global Leviathan to amend its hopeless status from this never-ending limbo. A similar consequence of the weakness of world authorities to act morally can also be applied to Taiwan, a de facto independent state, which few other countries have the courage to recognise. The big powers, especially totalitarian powers, are always very reluctant to recognise breakaway states. This is simply because they fear that such a recognition might encourage some of their own persecuted minorities to seek independence. It is for this very reason that the new independent state of Kosovo is still awaiting recognition by half the world.

No country in the world would currently have the courage to advocate this new definition of democracy. Our new definition has as one of its consequences the fragmentation of the world into numerous different states. There are no countries that would risk the breaking up of their empires, and any individual country that recommended such a policy to other powerful empires would be treated as a pariah state and would be subject to trade and diplomatic isolation as a punishment. The global adoption of the new definition of democracy could only happen when the ability to wage large-scale warfare is restricted to the single authority of the Global Leviathan. Countries throughout the world will only be dragged towards this new world order after living through a global catastrophe which eliminates most of the world's population. Yes, we've probably got such a disaster to look forward to before we come to our senses.

Printed in Great Britain
by Amazon

45065066R00020